Of Ash & Fire

poems by

DJ Hill

Finishing Line Press
Georgetown, Kentucky

Of Ash & Fire

Copyright © 2022 by DJ Hill
ISBN 978-1-64662-900-8 First Edition
All rights reserved under International and Pan-American Copyright Conventions. No part of this book may be reproduced in any manner whatsoever without written permission from the publisher, except in the case of brief quotations embodied in critical articles and reviews.

ACKNOWLEDGMENTS

Eternal gratitude to longtime editor Jenniey Tallman; artist Susan Solomon for her stunning cover and interior art; Michael Bazzett, Julie Harper, Jennifer Pastiloff, Tom Pelissero, and Katrina Vandenberg for their eloquent blurbs; Kirsten Miles, Jeffrey Levine, and fellow writers at Tupelo Press 30/30 Project for their daily inspiration; and Finishing Line Press for graciously publishing this collection.

To family and friends who've supported this journey, my heartfelt thanks. And RAH, much appreciation and love~

Publisher: Leah Huete de Maines
Editor: Christen Kincaid
Cover and Interior Art: Susan Solomon
Author Photo: Dani Werner Photography
Cover Design: Elizabeth Maines McCleavy

Order online: www.finishinglinepress.com
also available on amazon.com

Author inquiries and mail orders:
Finishing Line Press
PO Box 1626
Georgetown, Kentucky 40324
USA

Table of Contents

The Rising 1
Scientists Baffled by Bizarre Behavior 2
van-i-tas 4
Garden Slug Rejects Drowning in NA Beer 5
Doorman Confirms The Football Team in Kohler,
    WI is Nicknamed "The Toilet Bowls" 6
Up Schitt's Creek 7
"It's Called Gaslighting" 9
A George by Any Other Name 11
The Next Stage 12
Unexpected Visitor 13
Imagine What You Desire 15
Set Yourself Free 16
Ode to a Hotel Makeup Mirror 17
This Day 18
At the Bend of Two Rivers Road 19
Aspens Wave Us By 21
Lift Up 22
Midnight Through a Hotel Window 23
He Armed Himself 24
What Chief Plenty Coups Might Have Said 25
Another Summer 26
For Her 84th Birthday 27
When Does Summer End? 28
To a Friend on the Eve of Her Move 29
After Bleezer's Ice Cream 31
Be the Healing 32
Limitless 33
Bio 34

*'Say a prayer for the wind, and the water, and the wood,
and those who live there, too.'*
—*John Denver*

The Rising

Five trees, turning leaves
gold, holding firm 'til winds switch
wooden bodies bare

Rapids running quick
river rocks tumbled by force
Dame Nature's fury

Acres charred by fire
soot smudged cliff face not erased
indelible print

Floating clouds of brown
smog just above the skyline
air too thick to breathe

Masses fleeing fire
searching for sanctuary
strike warblers perplexed

Mother Nature stressed
endangered species hunted
for what, human sport

Prairie grass brittle
sunbeaten glare, counting days
Earth begs for mercy

Scientists Baffled by Bizarre Behavior
in remembrance of Rachel Carson

During fire fog at the trailhead of Twin Peaks
National Forest, disoriented birds flock

to pavement—we hedge our bets on chipmunks,
scrappy creatures tempting fate, flattened daily

or escape, the smoke and climbing temps drawing
birds to hairpin turns, we brake in horror, their refusal

to move, react, retreat to the safety of pines or flight
Susceptible Wilson's Warblers, packed to head south

yet blinded by their plight, confused by the cold
an early freeze, the tease of migratory routine

But here we are, heading home, surviving
the treacherous mountain turns, the warblers and us

we used to know but now do not, we clock
movement as they face our two-ton intrusion

We stop counting as we swerve
unable to avoid their fragile frames, small thin bill

bright yellow body with olive back, gentlemanly
males sporting a French style black cap

While the orcas swimming from the Strait
of Gibraltar, ram boats and vessels

their environment altered, fifteen times
orca slammed into the stern, disabling

boats, breaking rudders, whistling loud
something to learn, they swim up

the coast like clockwork each September
chasing tuna into the Bay of Biscay, they

remember when sailors and vessels and buoys
gave leeway, now they thrash, yachts harass

their pods on a freeway of giving back ten-fold
the threat—chipmunks, warblers, the orcas,
we are humans—emptying oceans, raging fires
the thirteenth chime, each earthly shudder

a reminder, we are running out of time.

van-i-tas

>*noun.* a still-life painting of a 17th-century Dutch genre containing symbols of death or change as a reminder of their inevitability

Yellowed peels mask blackened nub
Bruised orbs ferment and stain
Beauty mellowed by flaccid spots
We, proffered a short shelf life

The apple doesn't fall far from the tree
Green can spoil the whole bunch
How soon appears the rot
But we all come to this, don't we

Domestication thwarts fruit, so don't
Upset the proverbial cart, no bearing tree
Immune, expect worms, if you crave
Spring, shake the tree, when ripe gives way

Is it true apples are always eaten
By nasty pigs in a poke, spoke of platitudes
Spurned by blossoms, decaying fruit
Clings to branch, unable to escape the fall

Garden Slug Rejects Drowning in NA Beer

Or at least that's what I told myself, seeing the nibbled
edges on an otherwise glossy, neon leaf, beer bait untouched.
One stayed out too late, the sun already breaking horizon,
his opaque body clinging to the pockmarked tendrils.

I had suspected the culprit was an earwig, a conundrum
of cryptic species, aka Pincer Bugs—do they really pinch?
But the two bodies bore no resemblance, as the leaves wilted
then dropped, a tell-tale sign the clematis was doomed.

An Australian once ate a diseased slug on a dare,
there the slimy slug slinked across the patio; blokes chugged
Little Creatures while Sam gulped the wretched mollusk,
lapsing into a coma for 420 days—

"I love you," the last words spoken to his mother.
While just last month a virus walked into a bar, lifted a glass
to 16 friends, exhaled plumes of garlic, curry, and alcohol, the spittle
of a super emitter, stealing himself away to another party, unscathed.

Unharmed, a similar slug ignores the Beck's, the absence of hops
and hungrily grinds his way up the trellis. "No more 3/2 beer," I
murmur, "time to serve up the BrewDog, 41% ABV, guaranteed
to leave slugs staggering"—a safer bet than a beer in a bar in the
summer of 2020.

Doorman Confirms the Football Team in Kohler, WI is Nicknamed "The Toilet Bowls"

He said it with a straight face
but I knew their season was
destined to go down the drain

Homecoming royalty—
the Princess with porcelain skin
a King on his throne
could do nothing but sit idly by

as the quarterback dodged left
swirled right, pausing only long
enough to pass to the tight end
with his extra rolls

and the cheerleaders yelled
"Push 'em back, push 'em back
waaay back!"

while the parched marching band
passed water around before
relieving themselves of their duties.

Up Schitt's Creek

Being it was Emmy night, we grabbed a
frozen pizza, bottle of Cabernet Franc
settled in with the Roses: Johnny, David,
Alexis, and the diva, Moira.

Lost in conversation, Moira's spilling her
dark side, Alexis, still clueless, she could
only stand by, David and Patrick, facing
quite a dilemma, slivered moon passing day

right after sunset, there came a low moan
lasting just a few seconds, the source of the
power at earth's core expended, towels in
washer, begging to dry, ceiling fan, stilled,

the spin interrupted. Our house, now quiet,
us with nothing to do, but wait out the silence
a dog at our heels, we padded to bed, flipping
light switches, fans, a breathing machine,

all of them dead. No daily sports scores,
candidate mishaps, or songs by Tom Petty.
Alexa the eavesdropper, usually chatty,
even she, now silenced, could not face

the music. New iPhone from Apple refusing to
function, the WIFI disabled, a poem past deadline,
words carefully crafted, held hostage in Dropbox,
googling generators, conspiracies, and worst of all

end times, hourglass spinning, the blank screen
of panic, what if, how long, contingency plan, frantic
steady tick of the clock, counting hours and
seconds, when suddenly it awakens, our agony

ended, as David, Alexis, Johnny and Moira with Emmys in hands, the other mimosas. Next time let's hope it won't come to this, darkness and drama tonight in Schitt's Creek.

"It's Called Gaslighting"

Not familiar with the term
I did a quick internet search
Google leads to Amazon
And the book *Gaslighting:*

*Recognizing Manipulative &
Emotionally Abusive People*

As if in the age of COVID-19
Massive unemployment, social
Unrest, we can break
Free, I clicked Buy Now, as now

My curiosity was piqued, in the next
7 hours and 45 minutes, *Gaslighting*
Could arrive via USPS, Wednesday
November 3rd at 3, and I too could

*Recognize Manipulative &
Emotionally Abusive People*

Gaslighting is available, new & used
Begging the question, did they master
Or identify the master manipulator
After Chapter 1 or back cover reviews

If you need further confirmation, it's
Recommended you bundle *Gaslighting*
With Recovery Notebook & *The Gaslight
Effect*: How to Spot and Survive.

Beware! He's witty, confident, controlling
Distractor of truth, liar, triangulator
Such as a politician who never admits
He could make a mistake

Reviews from Syndrella, Maggie Mae
and Janine Cope give him away
Give us a way if we accept
How vulnerable we really are.

A George by Any Other Name

Last evening, late, cursed by warrior Mars
going retrograde, a blood orange fire moon glaring
through my bedroom window, I found myself wide awake

and all that came to mind was Shakespeare's quote about
names—I thought of George, not a certain George or
by George, but any George who I might count like sheep.
So began an hour of attempting to lull myself to sleep with George:

Washington, Senior & Junior, King George the fifth
Gershwin, Harrison, Michael and Strait
Boy George, of course, Benson, Thorogood and Kennedy
There's Carlin, Clooney, Foreman, Hamilton, Lucas, Takei

And I, suddenly transported to Star Trek in the 60s: Spock, Bones
Uhura, Kirk, the Trouble with Tribbles, and beam me up
Scotty, which doesn't even start with G or have anything to do
with George. I corralled the crew back into Starship Enterprise

and started again: George Burns, Mikan, Orwell, Patton,
C. Scott, Jones, Soros, Floyd, Peppard, Phyllis, Curious, Jetson,
R. R. Martin led to thoughts of Westeros, dragons,
Khaleesi, Khal Drago, and Joffrey—the evil, wannabe king.

Finally, too tired, with no more Georges resting on the tip of my
    tongue
I rolled over to count sheep
refusing to name a single one.

The Next Stage

It starts early, suckers
Cars idling in drive-thru
Tubes vaporizing
Currency before your eyes

Hello Kitty—
Open your pretty purse
Let me see your stash
Coins collating into cash

Hey little girl, come on
Over, watch your money
Grow, it doesn't on trees
His voice saccharine sweet

Soon your curved bumpers
Park in the lot, the suits
Ask if you want it
Free checking, no strings

Attached, you're not
Except to freedom and fast
Cars, boys on hot summer
Nights, don't sweat it

Teenagers don't wait
They want it now, cash
Cards to feed into slots
How easy to give in

But get yourself
Protection, much needed
Attention, credit is
King.

Unexpected Visitor

So, the oddest thing
happened this morning
the third day
since the beginning
of a fall monsoon

I was sipping hot tea
lost in thought
watching rain weep
from the sky

When a female mallard
sauntered up my circle
drive, her handsome friend
waited in the wings

She waddled determinedly
as though she had something
to speak with me about
maybe to borrow a cup
of birdseed or invite me
to book club although
it might be unlikely we shared
the same taste in literature

Perhaps it was to complain
about the noisiness of my hens
or to protest their gossip-spreading ways

As she swung her tail feathers purposefully
en route to my front stoop
I imagined she was sporting
a stylish canary yellow handbag
tucked under her wing
a pair of puddle stompers
keeping her webbed feet dry

I cracked open the front door
fully expecting her to say,
"Good day, Miss Hill
May I join you for tea?"

Imagine What You Desire
after Jennifer Pastiloff

In the wake of a fresh new
morning, I open my eyes
to the wonder, forgetting that
heart pain which never subsides
but knowing your narrowed
eyes and fisted heart have softened.

The backpack of stones
emptied, I rise, spirit lightened,
humped back and slumped
shoulders straightened, this world—
despite its flaws and angst—draws me
to it, as a honeybee to swaying flowers
in shifting breeze, these are the faces
I desire: bright and attentive blossoms
who know no judgment; angling their
beauty to the light—accepting love,
care, mercy, understanding, forgiveness,
grace—forgetting the arrows
as I lay mine down.

This peace, our peace, will echo
through meadows, foothills, canyons,
climbing to the cragged summit, tossing
ashes on a path we will no longer tread.

Set Yourself Free

Happiness is a butterfly
oftentimes it dances by
always flying out of reach
flitting nature, lessons to teach

Until one day it lights on you
and you don't know quite what to do
Try to catch it, hold on too tight
before you know, it's out of sight

Perhaps you might sit back and say—
if it should land again one day
I'll keep it gently in my hand
enjoy the moment, its sifting sand

Ode to a Hotel Makeup Mirror

O, how I've avoided you—
with your sleek, polished beauty
flawless halo lighting, generously
proportioned drop-forged finish
You, the magnification of time, I've averted
your reflection on more than one occasion
except this morning, the first full day

of fall equinox, sun crossing the celestial plane
you on the cold, gray marble, waiting
expectantly for a moment such as this—
streamlined nickel base, antiskid
bottom and multifunctional face,
adjustable brightness, choice of single to 5x
uptightness, me, starting slow, recognizing
the woman in the round frame, looking
much the same, gaining confidence I braved
the swivel to zoom in and just as advertised,
I spied with my own weary eyes every pore,
wrinkle, and age spot, a lone hair
from my chin, highlighted roots, touch of gray
setting in, the feet of crows crowding
eyes and temple, two blue veins
crisscrossed, a constellation of wise spots

Thank you, hotel makeup mirror,
for your non-corrosive, double-sided,
100,000 hours of LED lifespan
Each crease a reminder—
how glorious this life has been.

This Day

So much of life is spent
waiting
longing
for the wellspring of peace
—bigger house, more money
more free time, less stressing
happier children, less suffering
missing all along the blooms
off to the side of the path—

the gentle song, free gifts of love
the being as I am
that is, after all, what we really have—

who we are
to give and receive
the blessing offered
everyday.

At the Bend of Two Rivers Road

we both had seen the same
raccoon, stiff along the roadside

his front and back legs crossed
as though he had just laid down
for a post-squirrel nap, plump

two-tone tail stretched out
like a bottle brush. "The guard-rail
must have trapped him," she said

his black mask resembling one
a burglar might wear, or me at bedtime
—us laying on our sides, feigning sleep—

while just down the road, turkey
vultures congregated: one, two, three, four
five on a ledge, bald heads, red skin

black plumage and beak, skilled scavengers
soon to take flight, snowbirds
on the berm, grunting and hissing

I debated shooing them off
lest they catch a whiff of roadkill
still warm a stone's throw away

repulsed by their vile habit
of regurgitating carrion. I went back
to the scene wanting to wrap

his lifeless body in a faux fur blanket
or rewind time to when he was foraging—
his tiny human-like hands clutching

a trout, anticipating the rainbow flesh
his long saunter home, the family
waiting for their evening meal.

Aspens Wave Us By

Labor Day weekend 2020
smoke drifts through Independence Pass,
a faint outline of mountain peaks—
sleeping giants soon to wake

Native grasses shifting to fall wardrobe,
summer blossoms void of color,
parched pines, thousands of timbers
toppled like toothpicks after an avalanche

A ribbon of what used to be river
red-tailed hawks hard pressed to find prey
121 degrees in LA today, wildfires stifling
the rebellious sky, Mother Earth, taking out her ire

The relentless stream of traffic
strangling arteries, F-150s towing
Raptors, overstuffed trailers,
Jeeps, ATVs, stacks of fat

bikes, grinding the Sawatch Range
hogbacks to rubble. Yellow-bellied marmots
double-dog-dare drivers to be aware
victims of a reign of error

Road closed. Detour. Yield, travelers—
we've lost our guard rail, a runaway
circumstance destined to shift or fail
A modern-day circus-train

with us still on board. We,
the caged beasts, foaming
at the mouth, bending the bars,
nature's rules we can no longer ignore.

Lift Up

Rush hour is an anomaly in my new hometown—
population and elevation roughly the same: 6000;
sleepy mountain hideaway with Mt. Sopris, mother mountain
holding vigil, red and white foothills division, a legendary curse—

but Mondays at 4:30 the cars, drivers, stories, lives of every
shape and size line up for food bagged, plastic stacked
cookies, donuts, cakes and bread, while three blocks away
vacant bistro with white tablecloths and flatware set

in the mountains, a nip in the air, bracing for an unforgiving
season, sailboat on lift stranded, contentious election looms,
extended table truck with trailer, unloaded, five loaves
for the many, maybe with enough hands, pretending

Men and women checking in, volunteers approach car windows—
ask, "1, 2, or 3 bags?" A procession of lifetimes winding through
this asphalt parking lot, I recognize a few, they are me and you—
white skin, brown, hair up or down, old and new cars, raw

and healing scars, a few more days to hang on, the small boy with
mask donned, scuffed sneakers on tip toes, peeks expectantly at
risen loaves, not here for bagged groceries but to offer like
mom and sister, leaning into windows, 1, 2 or 3 bags—hope

The slow roll of traffic; clipboards, checklists, small boy trusting
pit bull baring teeth, one more car, back bumper missing, a man
on bike another on foot, no wheels to tread

This is America.
This is America.
This is America.

Midnight Through a Hotel Window
    for Charles Simic

Downtown Minneapolis, mid-September, red tower
of Hyatt eerily glowing, menacing, neon Fast Sign
3/4 Christmas strand swagged, spotlights, single
bulb swinging bare, man in his window unable
to sleep, another drinking wine, rocking his
leather recline, streetlights, a reflection of
pillars in darkened windows, occasional
car on the boulevard, a wall of photos
neatly framed, the homeless staking
claims to benches, under awnings,
asleep but not sleeping, backpack
on, one eye open, cops walking
their beat, child running wild,
parents weary begging sleep,
moving on, the next window
dark, then psychedelic colors
of purple and green, mother with
stroller, no baby seen, patchworked
panes, devoid of life, empty parking lots
lit, shadows of movement, a woman back
with shopping cart wobbly, figures in frames,
another light on, square after square lifting can
to lips, two boarded up windows, blur of images,
silent screens, unwinding in his easy chair, another
drink, neighbor back in kitchen, 100-watt is blazing,
glancing out, lifts glass to air, toasting my blank stare

He Armed Himself

Left a home
        like yours
walked onto
a campus
        like yours
passed faces
        just like yours

And while God clutched
His heart
angels shielding
        their eyes
he unloaded
evil and demons

he couldn't contain
        bloodstained sidewalks
        bloodstained brick walls
        blood on his hands and ours

carnage under
a merciless sky

What Chief Plenty Coups Might Have Said

Muted winds sweep across
prairie plains, rustling
coppery bones of ancestral
spirits dwelling in air

Pristine waters christen
chaste souls, yet untouched
by war or age or time
a holy crucible

Delicate blossoms inhabit
native fields with an earthen
palette of maize, cerulean, blood red
gifts of grandmother earth

But storm clouds gather
darkened spirits, harbingers
of arrows and spears, cast
from one born free of fear

Tribal remains cannot be silenced
nor the will of their god erased
the raven will return to redeem
that which the white man tried to take

Dedicated to my grandmother Beatrice Sliter Kreis, a missionary to the Crow Indians in Hardin, Montana, and to her daughter—my mother Margaret—who continues to share the stories of Chief Plenty Coups.

Another Summer

It happens every year about this time, my mother,
daughter, and I exchange texts—something like
Thinking of you, or *Miss him even more
this year,* and today, 25 years since your Dad died.

Whenever September rolls around, Dad is
already on our minds, Saturday evening the 16th,
shortly after the dinner hour, his pace-maker heart
stopped; Dad breathed his last as Mom held hers.

Today is cloudless but cool, fall bearing down—
an inevitable speeding train, mid-September sun
still soothing yet our backyard fountain is running low,
the perennial garden losing its brilliance, neighbor

children off to school, another gray hair spotted
in the teeth of our combs, Mom soon turning 88,
spending summers on the lake she and Dad visited
before marriage, children, grandchildren,

cancer, this afternoon Mom watched as hired hands
float sections of dock to shore, stacking piece
upon piece, their rubberized waders keeping
limbs from blueness, weathered beach chairs

tucked in as are horseshoes, grilling tools,
inflatable innertubes, swimsuits from the line, dry
I can see Mom standing on her deck, perhaps
in her blue jogging suit, her hair just so,

overseeing this year's extraction of summer
and I wonder if it is Dad she sees, his late season
tan, beads of perspiration as he lifts the heaviness.
Our childhood dogs running back and forth

across the shore, barking wildly at the setting sun.

For Her 84th Birthday

my mother-in-law requested
a poem where she wins
the 2020 FedEx Cup

and I replied, "Sure, I can make
that happen," the poem I mean
as the FedEx Cup only allows

men, my mother-in-law watches
religiously, her favorite golfers
wedded to the game, not ego

which is why I could see her, Angie
striding onto the course—white jeans
her favorite baby pink collared shirt

matching shoes, arthritic hands grasping
Big Bertha, as the men stand clear
of her swing, determination, she strolls

confidently down the course, offering
sage wisdom, complimentary chocolate
chip cookies to her caddie, her grandson's

age, pointing out the subtleties
the acronym of GOLF—gentlemen
only, ladies forbidden—the irony

of an 84-year-old mother of five
spending her weekends watching
predicting who will take home

the trophy, the earnings, the glory
in my mind 36-year-old Dustin Johnson
is replaced by my mother-in-law.

A girl can dream.

When Does Summer End?

Hard to say in the dark
days of COVID-19
Summer, the season that leaves
us wanting more

When my children were young
they spent the waning hours
as if they were their last,
fledglings ready to take flight

Labor Day weekend we packed in
bike rides, mini golf, barbecues
in the shade of the sugar maple,
soon to turn, but holding its breath

Bare feet running through freshly cut
grass, watermelon, the last taste of freedom
Days when loving your child
seemed enough

Tonight, parents pack lunches, insist
on a reasonable bedtime, call too many
times for kids to leave their dusk play
for bath and bed, one more time

Tomorrow, the reminder of the sun
will wake them, us, to a new paradigm
Board buses, venture into classrooms
brave whatever comes next

We watch as they enter another
realm, move just beyond our grasp
We didn't know then—
these were the best of times.

To a Friend on the Eve of Her Move

You might be interested to know—
according to a therapist and friendship
researcher—that making friends at our
age is a particular challenge, the circle of
potential candidates slowly dwindling each year
add distance, a pandemic, economic hardship
and no one wanting to leave the safety
of home, alert to germs, masks, and
social distancing, the good news being,
according to the researcher, that
friendship has become more hands-off,
not having to go through the hassle
of meeting at a coffee shop, playgroup
or bus stop as we did when our children
were young, now grown, these sacred
spaces reserved for the next generation,
but lucky for us we can turn to Hey!
Bumble, VINA, Meetup, and MeowChat
friendship apps—Over 60 dot com says this is how
we grow our legion of fellow sexagenarians
in three easy steps: Admit our desire to
reinvigorate our social life, make friendship
a priority, and commit to 'getting out there
to make the first move,' somehow finding
a friend in 2020 resembles speed dating
and if we have questions or need support,
Over60 is a keypad away—
how ironic, friendship evolving to the
click of a button

Which is why, Alice, tomorrow
as you hit the open road, house sold,
belongings stowed, baby grand in
temperature-controlled—I want you

to know I will do none of these things
to replace your warm smile, the ease
of our coffee chats, your uncanny ability
to check in at the perfect time, someday
soon you will land, reunite with your baby
grand, in a new space, never forgetting
Red Mountain or Buck Prince, listening
under whispering pines, as you serenade
with a song you know by heart

After Bleezer's Ice Cream
    To Bob on our 11th anniversary

I am a pensive poet
I write poems by the score
today's our anniversary
and I'm here to write one more

Some say love is fleeting
Some say love's divine
I know love from lovers past
from Eden throughout time

Ginger Rogers, partner Fred
Bergman, Bogart, Bacall instead
Prince Rainier and Princess Grace
Monaco their hiding place
Romeo and Juliet
even Adam hedged his bet
Antony's Egyptian queen
George and Gracie stayed a team
Abigail, John, June and Johnny
Hepburn, Tracy, Nancy, Ronnie,
Mr. Darcy, Lizzy Bennett
Forrest Gump, he knew what love meant
Hazel Grace, Augustus Waters
Ryan, Hanks, Grant and Roberts,
Rachel, Jacob, Boaz, Ruth,
love can last when based on truth

I am a playful poet,
I write poems by the score
today's our anniversary
and I am here to write one more.

Be the Healing
> *On collaborative writing in 2020*

You there, with beating heart and sacred breath—
whose touch is missed but presence felt—take my hand
and extend yours to another, a human chain with
the power to mend, to move, to change.

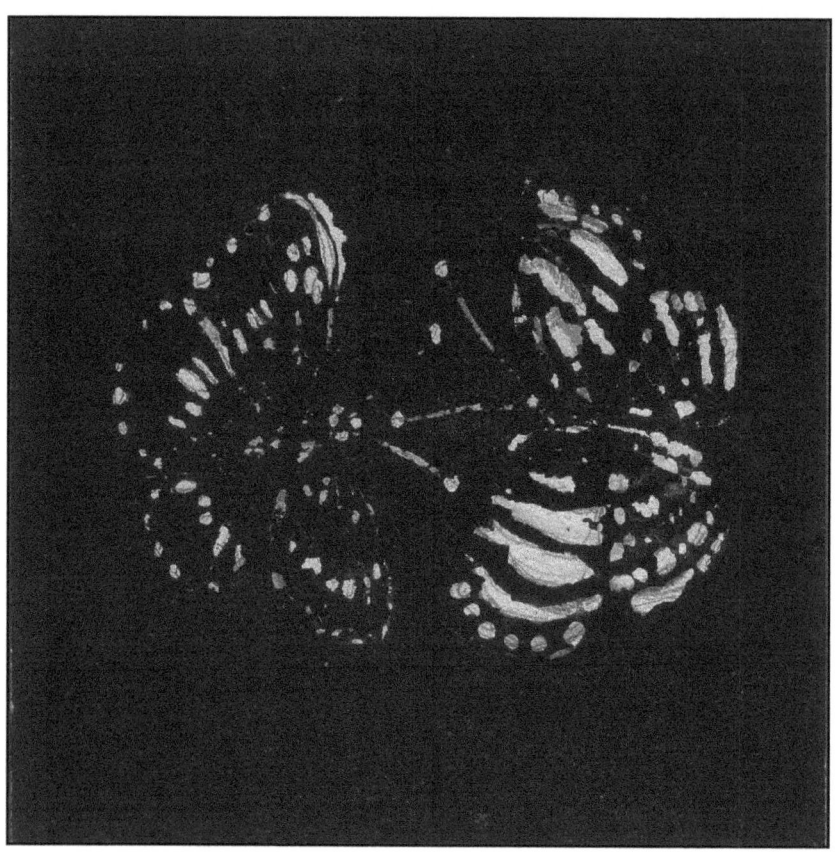

Limitless
> *A utopian themed Renga by the 30/30 September poets[1]*

What I'm really trying to say is:
Fuck transcendence! I will gladly risk
Our imminence, our riotous re-
                            calibration.
It will change you from within,
cell by cell, until you're free.

Soul beyond pleasure,
earthbound, kneeling at the edge,
dirt as offering.
Our hands, hearts, opened and outstretched
Gathered truth freely tossed to the limitless sky

More stars than we can see:
Orion's tunic, club, and shield
thrown off, put down for good.
Anchored in fallible flesh,
we find buried communion.

edges are relative
the places we touch to find
the middle balance heart blood
We will watch Orion cross the sky at night,
We will listen to the wind muss the treetops.

Flesh of the moon, eat
sap of the trees, drink deeply
here, this is for you.

---

[1] This Renga was a collaboration of nine poets used with permission by Louise Akers, Kris Bigalk, Lucia Galloway, Raki Kopernik, Michelle Lesifko-Bremer, Kindra McDonald, Doug Van Gundy, and Liza Wolff-Francis

DJ Hill's debut collection of poetry and collage, *Homespun Mercies,* won the IBPA Benjamin Franklin, NYC Big Book, and CIPA EVVY Awards in Poetry, and was a silver medalist in the Nautilus and IPPY Book Awards. It was recently named a winner in the Art category and finalist in the Medal Provocateur, First Horizon, and Grand Prize Short List of the Eric Hoffer Book Awards. The cover art, her piece Release, was named Spirit of the Suffragists at the opening ceremony of VOTE: A Centennial Celebration at the Loveland Museum in Loveland, CO.

Her poetry and mixed media art have appeared in *The Rumpus* and numerous magazines, journals and anthologies including *Worcestershire Poet Laureate, JOMP 21's Dear Mr. President, Gone Dogs: Tales of Dogs We've Loved,* and most recently in the spring issue of *Analogies and Allegories Literary Magazine.*

Who's That I Hear, DJ's first children's book, was released April 6, 2021.

DJ holds a BFA in creative writing from Hamline University in St. Paul, MN. She writes and creates in her studio in Santa Fe.

www.ingramcontent.com/pod-product-compliance
Lightning Source LLC
Chambersburg PA
CBHW050821090426
42737CB00022B/3469